CCSS Genre Realistic Fiction

 **Essential Question**
How do people uncover what they have in common?

The Best Friends' Birthdays

by Diana Noonan

illustrated by Burgandy Beam

Chapter 1
Party Plans................................2

Chapter 2
Party Panic................................5

Chapter 3
Party Time...............................10

Respond to Reading............................16

PAIRED READ The Same but Different.............17

Focus on Literary Elements....................20

Chapter 1
Party Plans

"Snap!" Jodie said.

"Snap?" Prema's deep-brown eyes opened wide in puzzlement. She had been in America for three months now, and *still* she could not understand everything that her new best friend said to her.

"'Snap' is like when two things are the same," Jodie said, "so when you said your birthday was next week, I said 'snap!' because mine is, too."

"Our birthdays are having on the same week," Prema said, comprehension dawning.

"Happening," Jodie said. "They're *happening* in the same week." They laughed together, and then Jodie's face lit up.

"Hey, we could have a joint birthday party, maybe a slumber party at my place because we have plenty of room, and we could have pancakes, and …" Finally noticing the blank look on Prema's face, her friend stopped to explain. "A slumber party is when you invite friends over and they stay overnight."

Prema's eyes sparkled with excitement. Some things she just could not understand, such as why her father, who had been a nurse in their small town in India, had to take more exams to be a nurse in America; or why, in this new country, cucumbers came wrapped tightly in plastic! But a shared birthday party she *could* understand, and at the thought of it, her stomach tingled in anticipation.

"We should make a list and write on it the names of all the people who are coming to the slumber party," Prema suggested, proud of the way the new expression slipped out so smoothly. Jodie grinned and handed her a piece of paper and a pen.

"Grandmother Madhabi," Prema said aloud as she wrote. "She must come first on the list, and then my uncles and aunts, although of course so many are still in India."

"You're asking your *grandmother* to a *slumber party*?" This time it was Jodie's turn to look perplexed.

Prema's expression suddenly became very serious. "Yes, of course. She *must* attend, and all my uncles and aunts and my cousins. And my mother will also ask her friends, and my father will ask his, and—"

Jodie groaned. "Prema, there's no way that all those people will fit into the house, and anyway, a slumber party is just for kids. I mean, no adult is going to want to sleep on the floor with a bunch of kids shouting and laughing all night, are they?"

"But my relatives always come to my birthday," Prema said, looking bewildered.

"Well, same here," Jodie replied, "but we invite them at a different time. Gramps and Gran come over for dinner on the actual *night* of my birthday, and my auntie and uncle and cousins usually come by sometime that week. But none of them comes to my birthday *party*—not when my friends are here."

Prema felt the tingle in her stomach turn into a lump. "Ohh, I am so tired of getting things wrong," she thought, "and I was so sure that birthday parties were the same here as in India."

She swallowed her embarrassment and decided that she would not let her mistake spoil things. "I am living in America now, and I will learn how to do things Jodie's way, and a slumber party is a perfect idea," she thought.

She picked up the pen and firmly wrote "Latisha" at the top of the page, and then she added "Lynn, Renee, Carmen."

Jodie grinned, and the two friends began to talk about how they would decorate the invitations and what music they would play, squabbling happily over each other's suggestions.

Chapter 2
Party Panic

"Ammu, I have something fantastic to show you," Prema said when she got home from school. She kicked off her shoes at the door and waved the party guest list, but her mother was distracted by her bag of produce.

Ammu pulled out a fragrant red and gold fruit and flourished it triumphantly. "Fresh mangoes, so that we can make your favorite *lassi*. It will be just like at home."

"Yum," Prema responded automatically, her mind still on the party. All the ideas and plans that she and Jodie had made came tumbling out as her mother prepared the yogurt drink. She was so excited that she couldn't stop chattering even as Ammu's expression altered from interest to worry.

"And all these girls—they will be wearing their night garments to this … this *slumber* party?" Ammu said hesitantly, as if she could not believe what she was hearing. "And your grandmother is not to be invited, nor your cousins and aunts and uncles?"

When Ammu said it aloud like that, Prema started to feel worried, too—worried that she wouldn't be allowed to have the party at Jodie's house.

"I think that your father will object most strongly to this slumber party," Ammu continued. "He will be home very late tonight, so we will talk about it tomorrow."

Prema lay in bed that night worrying about Baba's reaction to the party plan. She had always had a good rapport with her father, although since they had come to America, he often worked long hours and they did not spend as much time together. "I cannot wait until he passes his exams," Prema thought. She knew that this was his greatest anxiety.

In the morning, Baba looked tired, and Prema was afraid that asking him about the celebration would make him angry. But when she mentioned it, he just folded his arms tightly across his chest and said, "No."

"No?"

"It is absolutely out of the question. You cannot wear your nightclothes outside of this house, and how can you sleep away from home when we are not with you?"

"Baba, it is what everyone does here—" Prema began, but her father had not finished.

"What would your grandmother and aunts and uncles think of us if we did not invite them to your birthday? You have not thought of these things at all, Prema."

Prema blinked back her tears. Baba had made up his mind, and there was not an ember of hope.

Jodie was more confident, though. "I have an idea," she said when the two girls were walking to school together, but she wouldn't say what it was.

That evening after Prema and her parents had eaten dinner, the doorbell rang. Prema opened the door, Ammu hovering behind her, and found Jodie standing outside with her mom and dad.

"Mrs. Banerjee, I've brought my parents to talk to you and Mr. Banerjee," she announced with a polite but determined look on her face.

At first Prema felt uncomfortable to be in the living room with Jodie's parents and Ammu and Baba all smiling at each other but saying very little.

Then Jodie's mom spoke. "A slumber party must seem rather strange to you, Mr. and Mrs. Banerjee," she said. "I guess moving to a new country has required a big adjustment."

"Oh, we have parties in India also, but *we* do not allow our young girls to run around the neighborhood in nothing but their nightclothes," Baba said.

Jodie's dad assured him that the girls arrived in their party clothes and only put on their pajamas when it was time for bed.

"In our family, it is also not usual for children to sleep away from their parents unless they are staying with relatives," Ammu added.

Jodie's mom smiled. "I don't know how you'll feel about this suggestion, but we could always shift the slumber party to *your* house if that would help. Then Prema wouldn't have to sleep away from home."

Prema could see that Ammu liked the idea of hosting the slumber party, but her father had another concern. "A birthday is very important in our community because it reunites all the family and friends. We do not think these adults will be happy with this *slumber* idea."

"I'm sure they wouldn't," Jodie's dad responded dryly, and then he told Ammu and Baba that when one of their children had a birthday, they asked family friends and relatives to come over at a different time.

Baba nodded, and Jodie's mom started talking again. "A slumber party is very easy if you rent a family movie for everyone to watch, and an activity is fun, too—in fact," she said, looking at Ammu, "I was wondering if you might like to paint the girls' hands with henna."

"Oh, I would be happy to do that, and Prema can help, too," Ammu said.

"We could make the food together and have a combination of Indian and American party food," Jodie's dad suggested.

"And I'd love to come over in the morning and help out with the pancake breakfast," Jodie's mom offered. "That is, if you want me to."

Ammu looked at Baba, and Prema looked at Jodie. The girls held their breath and waited. It seemed to Prema as if they waited forever before Baba spoke. His voice was very quiet.

"I think that we are living in America now," he said. "Some American things we do not understand, but we want Prema to be happy, and perhaps this slumber party will be acceptable if the children can come to our home."

Ammu smiled at Jodie's parents. "Prema's teacher says that Jodie has been a kind mentor to our daughter, and we are very grateful. She is a good girl."

Prema was so delighted that she almost jumped up and down, but she kept as calm as she could. When Ammu went into the kitchen to make tea for everyone, Prema went, too, and carried the cups into the living room.

"Thank you, Baba," she said as she set the cups down on the table. She spoke very clearly so that everyone could hear her, and then she gave Baba a kiss on the cheek.

"We are very proud of our daughter," Baba told Jodie's parents. "Prema is a good girl, just like your Jodie."

Chapter 3
Party Time

The week before the party, Jodie and Prema set to work to produce the invitations, sprinkling them with glitter and writing the details in their tidiest handwriting. Their parents had agreed that they could each invite five friends.

Prema laughed when Jodie said that she had never had such a big birthday party before. "Actually, I am thinking that this is a very little party," she said. "If you live in India, the relatives are many, and then there are the family friends and the school friends as well!"

On Prema's birthday, her grandmother was in the kitchen when she came home from school, and there was a large, flat box on the table.

"Nani!" said Prema.

"*Namaste*, my Prema," said Nani, hugging Prema tightly. "Here, open your present."

Inside the box was a beautiful new *salwar kameez,* teal blue with the pants covered in silver dots.

"Thank you, Nani, I will wear this at the party," Prema said, rubbing the soft fabric against her cheek.

"Your mother tells me that you are having many friends to sleep at your house on Saturday night," her grandmother said, her eyes gleaming mischievously.

Prema nodded, and Nani smiled broadly. "I am very pleased that we are having your *real* birthday today because there would be too much noise for me at the slumber party!"

On Saturday afternoon, Jodie's mom and dad arrived to help prepare the food while Baba went to the Indian DVD store to choose a movie for the party.

"Please, Baba, get the new one about the nomadic prince and the singing camel," Prema called. "My friends in India say that it is very funny," she told Jodie. "What did you bring?"

"I brought a comedy, too," Jodie replied. "This is going to be one hilarious party!"

Ammu was already cooking, emptying a can of condensed milk into a pot and stirring it around and around.

"My mother is making *laddu*," Prema explained. "They are delicious coconut sweets just like truffles, and we always have them on my birthday."

"Do you mind if I cut up this roll of cookies and bake them in your oven?" Jodie's dad asked as Ammu put the pot aside and handed Jodie's mom a tray for the pizzas.

"My kitchen is your kitchen," Ammu said, smiling.

Just before five o'clock, the girls went to Prema's room to change into their new party clothes. Prema spun in front of the mirror, enjoying the glitter of her salwar kameez and the soft chime of the bracelets on her wrists. Jodie spun around, too, to check out her new skinny jeans.

"The balloons! We've forgotten the balloons!" Baba said as the doorbell rang. "Where did I put that … that object?"

"You mean the balloon pump?" Jodie's dad asked, grabbing it from the chair, and the two men began blowing up the balloons as the first party guest stepped into the room.

Before long the house was filled with people.

"Aren't the adults supposed to go home?" Prema asked at six o'clock when most of the moms and dads were still at the party.

"They usually do, but I think the party food looks too interesting, and they don't want to leave," Jodie's mom said.

"Let them stay for supper," Ammu said. "The adults can eat in the kitchen and the children in the living room. There is plenty of food, and this is how we like it—many people, adults as well as children. It is the Indian way."

Prema was so busy answering everyone's questions about what they were eating that she almost forgot to have some party food herself.

In the kitchen, Ammu was explaining how to make *kosha mangsho* to a group of parents. "I had to go to an Indian delicatessen for the mutton," she said. "But the *luchi* is just made with white flour, so it is very easy. Come over some time and let me show you."

During supper Prema glanced around for Baba, but she could not see him anywhere. She hoped he wasn't feeling uncomfortable with so many strangers in the house. She went looking and found him hunting through a sturdy cardboard carton in the garage.

"What are you looking for, Baba?" she asked.

"The movie camera," he replied. "I want to present your grandparents in India with a movie of our new American life. If I do not take it soon, all the guests will be wearing their nightclothes, and it would never do for Dadu and Thakurma to see that!"

Prema giggled. "No, that would be terrible."

It was after eight when the last parents left, and Jodie and Prema helped carry the leftover party food into the kitchen as the other girls changed into their pajamas.

"Are you coming back to help make pancakes for breakfast?" Jodie asked her parents.

"Would you like us to?" Jodie's mom asked Ammu, who gave a spurt of laughter.

"Yes, you *must* come to show me how to make American pancakes," she said as her shoulders shook with the joke. "Because if you do not, the children will have to eat green chili *rasam* and rice—that is what we have for breakfast!"

"Don't worry," Jodie's mom said, laughing now, too, "we'll be here bright and early!"

Summarize

Use details from *The Best Friends' Birthdays* to summarize how Prema and Jodie's families uncover what they have in common. Information from your graphic organizer may help you.

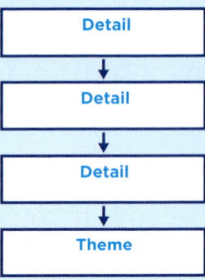

Text Evidence

1. How can you tell you that *The Best Friends' Birthdays* is realistic fiction? **GENRE**

2. What is the theme of this story? How do the discussions between the two families about a shared birthday party help to communicate the theme? **THEME**

3. What is the meaning of the word *object* on page 5? What is another meaning for *object* as it is used on page 12? What clues in the text helped you determine which meaning to use on each page? **HOMOGRAPHS**

4. Jodie and Prema come from different family backgrounds. Write about the events in the story that show that even though they come from different cultures, they have a lot in common. **WRITE ABOUT READING**

CCSS Genre Realistic Fiction

Compare Texts
Read about two girls who learn about the foods of their different cultures.

The Same but Different

School is out; Rosa and I are running,
dodging past the others at the gate.
Her parents are out this evening,
and she's coming over for dinner.

Up the garden path,
the delicious smell of spices
usually makes me happy
that I'm home.

But today I don't know what to think;
I'm watching Rosa's face.
A meal here won't be
what she has at her house.

"Priyanka, Rosa!
Come help with dinner,"
my mom calls from the kitchen downstairs.

I peel potatoes;
my mom shows Rosa
how to chop hot peppers,
but she already knows
from when her dad cooks chili.

Garlic and butter
sputter in the pan.
"It's like when Mom cooks *frijoles*," Rosa says.
But then we add the spices,
and the air is full of flavor.
"But different," Rosa adds
as we listen to the crackle
of mustard seeds popping in the heat.

Soon it's time to eat,
and we're off to set the table.
I'm sure now that Rosa
won't mind the spice.

With Dad and Sanjay
sitting around the table,
we load our plates
with tasty, spicy food.

Then I look around and realize
we're the same as any family
sitting together, sharing a delicious meal.
The same but different.

Make Connections

Why is Priyanka worried about Rosa coming to her house for dinner? ESSENTIAL QUESTION

In both *The Best Friends' Birthdays* and *The Same but Different*, how does food help reveal the fact that the people described have a lot in common? TEXT TO TEXT

Focus on Literary Elements

Foreshadowing Writers often build interest by giving their readers hints or clues about what is to come later in the story. This is called foreshadowing. Like a shadow that can be seen on the ground in front of you when the sun is behind you, the clues in a story can be seen before the real outcome is revealed.

Read and Find The author lets us know that Prema and Jodie are going to have some problems with the party because of their cultural differences. As readers we wonder what is going to happen. Through the story, the author reveals new problems, each one foreshadowing the solution.

Look for the first of these clues on page 5 when Prema's mother raises objections to the girls' party plans. Reread the story, looking for other problems that threaten the party, and the solutions that together make the party a success.

Your Turn

With a partner, choose a short story that you can read together. Take turns reading the opening passages aloud and pause to discuss any clues you notice that foreshadow what happens next. Finish reading the story to find out what actually happens. Did the clues help you predict the outcome?

Try to use foreshadowing when you next write a story or plan a video. It's a great way to hold an audience's attention.